Kiss/Hierarchy

POEMS BY
ALEXANDRA VAN DE KAMP

RAIN MOUNTAIN PRESS
NEW YORK CITY

First Printing August 2016

Kiss/Hierarchy
Copyright 2016 © by Alexandra van de Kamp

ISBN 978-0-9968384-0-5

Book design by:
David G. Barnett
Fat Cat Graphic Design
fatcatgraphicdesign.com

Rain Mountain Press
www.rainmountainpress.com
New York City

Printed in the USA

Cover Art: Janelle Cordero, "Abstract Blue"

For William

KISS/HIERARCHY

TABLE OF CONTENTS

I.   Bonjour Tristesse

II.   Nightgown

III. Dear Horologist

ACKNOWLEDGMENTS

The author wishes to thank the editors of the publications in which these poems first appeared, sometimes in an earlier version, or are forthcoming:

10x3 plus: "Bonjour Tristesse," "Marriage," and "Dear Key Largo"

32Poems: "A Caribbean Calendar" and "Lost Earring"

AMP: "Comparisons"

Arsenic Lobster: "Mrs. P. Goes House-Hunting" and "Head Cold"

The Boiler: "Nightgown" and "Today I am Not"

Cider Press Review: "Sleep: An Update" and "The Electrician"

The Cincinnati Review: "Kiss/Hierarchy"

Connecticut Review: "Still Life with Asparagus and Red Currants" and "No. 37/No. 19 (Slate Blue and Brown on Plum)"

Court Green: "Dear V—"

Denver Quarterly: "A History of Apples"

Jet Fuel Review: "The Swill of Sleep," "Poem with a Train in it Traveling to Constantinople," and "Poirot"

Lake Effect: "Le Pont de Passy et la Tour Eiffel," "Dear Teresa Wright," "My Life as a Dessert," and "How to Build a Summer Vacation" as "How to Build Your Own Summer Vacation"

Long Island Quarterly: "Suspended Breath"

Meridian: "Dear A—," "Dear L—," "Dear S—," and "Dear Horologist"

The National Poetry Review: "Dear Jean Seberg," "Miss Marple Solves the Mystery of the World," and "Dear B—"

The Prose Poem Project: "How to Survive Yourself: Nine Steps" as "Nine Steps on How to Survive Yourself"

Red Rose Review: "A Scandinavian Hotel in Couplets" and "I've Decided to Write the Greatest Poem in the World."

River Styx: "Upon Returning from our Tenth Wedding Anniversary Vacation"

The Southampton Review: "Miniature Secretary Incorporating a Watch (1766-1772)"

Thrush, A Poetry Journal: "Excavation" as "Archaeology" and "Tulips are Found to be One of the Most Delicious Foods for the Animal World"

Some of these poems previously appeared in the chapbook, *Dear Jean Seberg* (2011), winner of the 2010 Burnside Review Poetry Chapbook Contest. Some poems also appear in *A Liquid Bird Inside the Night* (2015), a chapbook published by Red Glass Books. "Mrs. P. Goes House-Hunting" and "Dear B—" were featured on *Verse Daily*. "Sleep: An Update," "Head Cold," "Bonjour Tristesse," "Marriage," and "Dear Key Largo" were all nominated for Pushcart Prizes. "A Scandinavian Hotel in Couplets" received a 2014 Best of the Net Nomination.

"To live, you must be drunk on something: Love. Money. Success. Failure. Even Whiskey. But Something."

—Pablo, the gambler in *Bonjour Tristesse,*
directed by Otto Preminger

BONJOUR TRISTESSE

LE PONT DE PASSY ET LA TOUR EIFFEL

— Marc Chagall (Oil on Canvas 1911)

Circus clown + rouge-cheeked whore =
the color scheme for this city scene.

It's France, of course. Pass the soup,
sing yourself to sleep and watch a river

murder itself again and again, the waters
churning in their own tureen of sunset blood,

the eye sucked along as if dragged
down a drain—some internal plumbing

in the paint pulling you toward the back
of the scene, where The Eiffel Tower waits,

the faucet turning off and on
all this luminous action, all this Technicolor

speed. The evening a migraine of pinks
and greens, or a clementine smashed

into sheer pulp and sheen. At the embankment
stands Chagall's blue and green horse—a flattened

gypsy caravan, a paisley toy in a child's
hopeful hand. Lurid fairy tale + working-class

arrondissement = a train shuttering across
the metal bridge—its blue windows blind eyes

in a peacock's sleeping tail. I'm waiting
for the gangster girl clutching her purse

to appear, skidding on heels beneath
the buildings simmering in reddish-

dark shadow, by the fiery brick walls
lining the river. Instead, no people in sight.

Instead, there is just the sky:
a crime of light and desire, a gash

of dark blue that whitens
as it recedes towards the Tower.

DEAR A—

Dear apple, dear angina,
dear after-thought, here is
another day that is not in August.
I write a friend who lives
in Berlin (not a city with an *a*
in it) and she doesn't respond. I think
of all the *strasses* in Berlin, all the cafés
with their sterling silver spoons and white,
weighted cups. Where does a city
actually end? Where does New York exactly
give way to the suburbs and stone-scattered
fields surrounding it? Once, walking across
Spain, I took note of how the pavement
gradually increased as we approached
the city's gates. Dear pashmina, dear
vintage year, it is so melodramatically green
this spring, I feel like I'm suffocating: insects
hatching eggs in the trees, the rain
dark as ink, the garden furniture stained
in cinematic regret. Where's Gatsby
the summer my mother was an extra
in the film? Newport mansions
oozing afternoon light, roses clipped
to the precise parting of lips. She wasn't allowed
to get a tan. Once the film was released,
I looked for her in a large party scene. Wearing a yellow,
lamp-shade dress, she was seated at a table,
barely visible through the dancing legs
of Redford and Mia Farrow.
Do plots end like cities, a little fed up
with themselves? But then some cities
are rosaries of tension. Dear abacus,
dear anxiety, thank god I am not

the boy in the Borges short story
who can never forget anything—his body
teetering on stone walls, his mind
tallying and tallying.

BONJOUR TRISTESSE

(for Jean Seberg)

Summer is a slippery sorbet, flavored
in lemon, raspberry,
or some other fruit-splashed shade. Bonjour
to the clairvoyant, rippling day.
It is 93 degrees in the shade,
but, hey, the shadows appear tame—
each shaped like a champagne glass
filling with something dark
and thrilling, something you can't
put a name to, although you have a feeling
it's naming you, as it drinks
up your arms, as it climbs
into the rooms you hadn't known
you kept inside of you. We are each
a portmanteau that life unpacks:
one compartment spilling out
into the voracious air, and then,
the next. You think your motives
are better than any other girl's? You think
you can pinpoint the exact place
at which intentions
tenderly wait? The heart
is a continent slipping inside,
or a Riviera about to slide and slide
into the Mediterranean—slack-jawed
and patient. Play the crap tables, heroine,
roll the dice, your taffeta dress skimming
past the gaming tables—in one hand
your gold-lamé clutch. The body
a champagne glass time twists
between index finger and thumb,
a nimble, shattering thing

we hate to see undone.
How far would you go
to hold onto what you presumed
was your own? *To own*
a verb with such a decisive,
ominous groan. Summer is a tray
upon which a medley of delicacies
is delicately displayed: in the morning
café au lait, in the evening, the sky
a crystal-ball blue. And,
my heroine, which pleasures
will you fight for, which hors d'oeuvres
will you choose?

DEAR TERESA WRIGHT,

(for Hitchcock)

Adolescence was never so milky
with unsure light, never so filtered
with small town ennui. Pull
at the threads in the bedspread,
girl-woman, mash the potatoes
before dinner, serve the soup
in its obedient tureen and wait
for your uncle to come, Fedora-hat
shadowed. Nothing is what it seems.
Watch how preconceptions shift
and tumble: newspaper clippings,
the library—ivy-covered and panic-
stricken—with its turrets and lit windows
going out one by one. You want to be
waltzed, held in tuxedo, cologne-
soaked arms, and instead you get detectives
photographing your house—your mother,
clueless and cracking eggs for the monotonous,
weekly cake. Afternoon, with its vague
intuitions and back-stair retreats, has come
sooner than you anticipated. Nothing
is what it seems. Waltz with me once, carry me
in your tender-gloved hands. Tunes
jump from one head to the next, and so
does dread—its hem dragging in
the claustrophobic mud. Your uncle takes you
to a smoky bar, tosses back a double scotch.
Be careful, woman-child, life can take over,
do with us what it wants. A marriage proposal
takes place in a dim, musty garage. Attempted
murder seems inevitable, the next note in your song's
tense, sexual scale. Thank God for passing neighbors,

thank God for second chances, but in this world,
no one leaves adolescence without a shiver of grief,
without the strangle-hold of what they once
thought was love slipping, just in time,
from their throats.

DEAR JEAN SEBERG,

Inspired by Barbara Bloom's "Homage to Jean Seberg, 1981"
—The International Center of Photography NYC,
January 18, 2008

Dear despair, dear Paris
sincere, whisper to me, tell me
a secret you can't repair. Newspapers
plummet like injured birds, cling
to my blond-haired arms. The elephant
immured in my dream last night
was helpless and tender-eyed. But what to do
with a several-ton pink body leashed
suddenly to your life? Where to put
such a weight? Above me, a curtain purrs
in an open window, flirting
with time and innuendo. Paris unfurls
like a sooty river, breathes helplessly
inside of me—the silver, stained wallpaper
bulging in my hotel room like a tumor. I hate
when someone states: "Live with no regret,"
when regret watermarks the heart, tattoos us
permanently to ourselves. The Japanese cherish
each crack in a broken vase, glaze the crevices
with gold. You can pay homage to anything
if you choose: black tar roofs, an apple browning
on a plate, as if blushing beneath your stare. No one
escapes this life without a history of some kind
rivering down their face and arms.
Hounded by the FBI, she was found dead
in a Paris car. Her youth a dimple
creasing the smoky waters of the screen. She seemed
all tossed-back bed sheets and cigarettes, all convertibles
and last-second decisions, but a late-in-life grief
seeped from those youthful, American fingertips.

Dear Paris, dear *café au lait*, I miss the *Ducados* in Spain—
their black tobacco filigreed the air, showed the breath
of those who were near.

KISS / HIERARCHY

There are two ways to reach me: by way of kisses or by way of the imagination. But there is a hierarchy: the kisses alone don't work.

—*Anaïs Nin*

If kisses don't suffice, their caviar salt and champagne
dew—what would? The night inside each kiss, the liquid bird

inside that night, the slick backs of ants sliding through the grass,
the moist reluctance of time inside a kiss, the standing back

and pondering the canvas of a kiss, its feast of unknowns—
its drowning flowers and rose dresses, its rising

barometers? Or the chaise-longue legs of a kiss, the pale face
emerging from a night-garden kiss. There are green-tea kisses,

kisses brewed long and slow, like the heat
building in trees in a Virginia June—the humid tapestry

of their branches, the swerved spine of their stare. A kiss
is never wrong. It knows what it is—whether it lies or

tells a truth. Each kiss is a museum hung with previous
kisses, a history: the Marc-Chagall kiss, the *View*

of Naples through a Window kiss. Windshield kiss, the
Let's get this over with kiss. Presumably, you could kill

with a kiss. It all depends on the setting and script,
on what needs to be done. A kiss is a dent

into us; it leaves its gun-powder smoke
and ash residue, its sparrows dropping from the sky.

Where does a kiss end and a scar
begin? Now I am getting all Ingrid Bergman on you.

All cat burglar and stealth bomber. But no movie
can tell you this. You have to kiss

your way through to your own truth
about a kiss; there is simply no other way

to do it. It's lonely. A kiss is a darkness,
a cave we fumble into

and through. But I only speak from
personal experience, from a wake

of kisses and not-kisses
trailing behind me, keeping me

in their own peculiar company.

STILL LIFE WITH ASPARAGUS
AND RED CURRANTS

—Adriaen Coorte (Oil on Canvas 1696)

Night falls diligently behind these pencil-long vegetables, these moon-

stairs. Eight to ten shoots bundled together. Pale and iridescent,

they night-sweat into themselves. Reddish-white at the tips,

yellow-white at the stalks, as if they were blushing upwards,

like shy debutantes at a ball. They are tender spears. Shredded tears

of expectation sulk, then evaporate off of them. Tipped upward,

each asparagus is a heaven-escalator, a humming contusion

of nervous white poised for the next step in the oil-slick firmament

the background has become for them, the one-way darkened window

they buoy in. They make a frosty bed; a dim, dew-soaked patch of lawn;

a hushed congregation lying there, forced into a strange patience

by the painter. They are the gray after-thoughts we have upon waking,

the last silvery gestures rising up from a dream. The missed chances

that accrue so quietly, which the heart dare not tally except

in the tenuous seam, the upward gleaming between sleeping and waking.

Like jelly fish in their ghostly, gelatinous stillness, their passive skimming over a darkness so much larger than them, they spill into what they know and don't know, these sinewy, star-fevered ladders, while the red currants drop in delicate bundles to each side of them—coins of ruby-blood trembling; sequined, sour skin bursting to be eaten.

DEAR KEY LARGO:

(for Bogart and Bacall)

If life were a hotel, it would,
at times, buck and swell. The temperature
is on the rise, the waves muddy
as regret and not receding. *Do you play the ponies?*
The long shot is only your wrists,
pale as snow and thrust out into the world,
a cacophony of small-time criminals
and masters of the fix; each man his own
version of a war—his hope faulty
as electrical wiring in a storm. And what
about the girls? They wait like potted plants,
they thrive only in the spotlight
of someone else's arms, but a few
sense the pressure dip and rise; like a barometer,
they take the world in stride. The shutters whack
and tremble, the hurricane lamps are in the shape
of tears. She's a widow and he's a wanderer,
the father's a cripple, and the gangsters
pace upstairs. Someone gets smacked around,
someone else dies with an unloaded gun
dropping from their hands. The wind ignores
the plot unfolding inside and tosses
the palm trees around like dice.
Gee, fella, can I have a drink? There's a singer
past her prime, her boyfriend the mob king
sweating upstairs. There's a widow and a wanderer.
That was a close shave. The local Native Americans
pound on the door, want out of the storm.
The ceiling fan spins like a headache
that won't end. What do you do with a gun's
black throat poking into your ribs? Funny

how a decision can tip when a little fear's
added into the mix. Hope is squeamish,
patriotism wary, and the mobsters
are peddling counterfeit money. Who, after all,
is the real public enemy? The gangsters
or your own thoughts, both equally capable
of holding you hostage. Meanwhile, Bacall
turns her face toward Bogart, and the camera stalls,
the hurricane subsides, and the pale flickering light
sliding across her cheeks would take a lifetime
to describe.

DEAR L—

Dear Lilliputians, dear Lily of the Valley,
dear Lisbon, the world grows grumpier
by the minute. Streets crack slowly
under my feet. My favorite pavement
was in Madrid: small cement squares
you could fit your life within—opaque,
sooty mirrors placed end to end.
At the grave, my grandmother's
tombstone had no end date. *I'll have to tell them*
to finish that out, my mother explains. Yet another
film noir in which the husband poisons his wife
with her warmed glass of milk each night—
rain falls heavy as rope in the final scene. It seems
love and violence breed and breed. Just now
the grass sleeps. The coffee was pale in Lisbon,
a light brown river cupped in my hands. We skipped
the museums. A balcony wrapped around the room
we were in. Statues crumbled against the sea-
bitten air. *I don't care, I don't care,* she declared.
To move the gears, the mechanic explained,
you'll need to ease the key forward in the ignition.
Dear Lily of the Valley—tilt your white bells
in the breeze. You were grandmother's favorite
flower, so don't sneeze! With each one, they say,
a shred of the soul escapes. *What to argue about*
next? The Lilliputians asked. My mother,
deciding what to give me, jewelry sprawled
on the white bedcover. She tugs free
of the velvet pouch a porcelain
mermaid. *This is from Copenhagen and was*
your grandfather's, she explains. In the novel
I'm now reading, the narrator, a drunk in India,
is slowly dying on the steps inside an apartment building.

The residents gingerly tiptoe by him. Not even
the cardamom and clove-spiced tea
they leave in a white steaming cup
can rouse him.

MARRIAGE

Let's skip the ribbons, the afternoon sky
eerie and metallic as desire, the grass
so damp it felt like a moistened sponge
beneath our feet—something that
could give way at any moment,
except it didn't. The violinist stroked
her strings and time mournfully
cascaded over us, seated in the pearl-
colored pews. It was a brother's wedding.
His white vest was embroidered
with swirls and meandering streams,
his shoes agleam. Rumors of tequila
in the sacristy before the ceremony
circulated fitfully. The bride bared
her tattooed shoulders like a duty—
her veil a voluptuous kite
bobbing down the back of her. I cried fat,
fruit-ripe tears, I cried translucent crystal balls
that melted down my cheeks, I cried
an afternoon and some cities. After,
the band tilted back their heads,
blowing their lives, and all that breath,
into their horns and sax, and we danced.
Dad was like Fred Astaire, we said,
while we swiveled our hips
and shook off our sweat. Outside,
the night fell like a dark room.
We stepped out to take in
some air, but found only saturation
and silence there. Back at the hotel,
Saturday Night Live did yet another
opening skit, but we turned off
the sound, wanted only to watch
the faces smile and twitch.

SUSPENDED BREATH

Nothing like a little x-ray
to tilt the world straight. The human body
more compressible than we care
to imagine as the technician squeezed
my breast in place and asked me not to breathe
for the duration. Nothing like suspended
breath to make you think. The world,
on a good day, a serene geometry
of trees and swerving roads, and the breasts:
two thick clouds curving clumsily
against the chest, a kind of weather inside
their gingerly-arranged globes—a kind
of snow falling and falling across the
x-ray film, (no Greta Garbo here,
sighing in the 1930's washed-out light
of her *Grand Hotel*,) but a terrain
the radiologist caresses
with her eyes and mind. Not for me
the dark cube of the radiologist's
room (so like the projectionist's booth
except this story includes you). Dr. Price
was the one (as if the universe
were having some fun) who set me free,
gave me the *okay* for another year.
It was December, the sky swirling
like a milky cup of tea, the roads
darkened by a recent, and now melted,
snow. Was it relief I felt? Or a certain jilt?
The close-call of it all just a little
too close? I drove out of the parking lot,
signaled to take a right, and hesitated,
watching the traffic thrumming by.

HOW TO BUILD
A SUMMER VACATION

Mine would begin with words like *innocuous* or

synesthesia. I would be reading *Madame Bovary* and learning

foreign words for clothes, such as *cravat* and *fez.*

There would be a smattering of dust, lavender-black dust,

as in the darkness under trees in a month of June,

exceptional for its cavalcades of rain. Fog would suffocate

cities in indecision, obscure the green islands offshore—

hallucinogenic arms embracing nothing.

In the silver glow of headlights,

the streets would grow wet and impatient. Raspberries

would buoy up from the *scratch and sniff*

cardboard garden in my hands. I'd press my nose

to my husband's skin and watch a salty tide

of bruised fog, a riverbed of unpicked fruit,

rise up to me. What mingles now

in that next room? The wallpaper in the hotel

had an antique, well-used odor; flowers

in rose and gold waltzed up and down our room.

The bathroom tiles were contact paper peeling up

under my toes. I want each day to pour like an hourglass—

svelte and methodical; loss encased

in a seasoned decanter and divvied out like a wine

brought up from a temperature-controlled cellar.

I want to be snagged thickly to something.

In the museum, in the painting, the woman's dress

in the summer garden radiated from across the room

like a halogen street lamp turning on at 6PM. The pointillist

beach scene grew more vivid at two hundred feet.

Clarity is just a matter of distance mixed with a massive

dollop of patience. On the ferry ride home,

we spied the island famous for its scientific experiments.

After, possums curled up along the side of the road—

gray, fleshy semi-colons—and we drove on,

trying to beat the storm.

POEM WITH A TRAIN IN IT
TRAVELING TO CONSTANTINOPLE

1.   A poem is saddled with breath, with its mints
and paprika. A poem is the Europe I zip on in sleep
like a dress: its well-thumbed tapestries, its
paint-chipped back alleys; the ever-present smell
of plumbing and espresso. It is the meandering dialog
that swims backstroke beneath my skin. It is my
Picasso striptease, my Josephine Baker
harem of sequins.

    A poem is a fussy, catch-me-if-you-can
geography. A Mediterranean sneering
with ions—the local flora fluttering
like some celebrity waving
her neatly-buttoned ivory gloves out of a car
tinted with second guesses. Only astute poems
make regret look attractive.

2.   And this poem? Is it made of fragrant summers
stitched with citrus mirrors? Rain kicking
a soft *can-can* against the window's pale
applause? Perhaps it's a B-movie replete
with indecisive heroine and casino-
art-deco gambling scene. A poem can be riddled
with make-up remover and leather satchels,
cerulean French boyfriends and pink plastic handcuffs.
It sashays with a line-up of bathing suits,
swaying against whatever you thought you might do
before the age of forty. It is a city
in ruins, the green sweating vines clawing your ankles
as you climb to the top of the collapsed
French fortress—the one with salmon-
striped lizards slipping across its stones
and an iron ship rusting like some lost cause

in the nearby ocean. I've decided
this poem has a plot and a cadre of rented Peugeots.
Also, a large black bird that blots out
the occasional cloud, its body a glossy cough
dividing the sky. Just now, someone hums to herself
a Viennese waltz. Her heart is a pale, hiccupy
pocket watch. She's on a train to Constantinople
accompanied only by her valise and a rushed litany
of unevenly-lit, magenta windows.

NIGHTGOWN

MISS MARPLE SOLVES THE MYSTERY OF THE WORLD
(á la the BBC)

You never know what awaits you

around the next corner. The body in the library

is dressed in lily-white taffeta. Each season,

another epidemic unfolds—be it emotional

or spiritual, a re-assorting of the heart

after we've come in contact

with that many more breathing souls. A person

is an incubator of sorts, a petri dish

of desire—each wish individual

as a fingerprint and skeptical

as a private eye. I'll never live

in a time period where women

unthinkingly slip on their elbow-length,

satin gloves. We all want what we came for,

just some of us want it more. The human face

is soft and malleable, and as inscrutable

as the tea leaves slushing about

at the bottom of the china cup

you are cradling now. Who wouldn't

want to drench themselves in the tawny,

half-light of a British dusk, the rain always

sniffling to itself somewhere

out in the audience? There's no World War I

in my past, no disillusioned fighter pilot. There are,

however, a slew of doubts, some uncanny

precipices, a burst, here and there,

of magenta azalea bushes, and a knack

for obsessing over details, just like any sleuth

on the hunt for clues. Your mind

is a gutter, Miss Marple, your judgment

a road refining its dark light

under the influence of an evening mist.

Come in, have a look around. We welcome you

into our parlor, we hope

you enjoy your stay at our house.

SLEEP: AN UPDATE

The body jackknifes—buckles like a dark road—
and each thought unfolds like relaxing
crumpled foil. The trees are detectives late
for a luncheon and checking their pocket watches.
It rains for the umpteenth time, like an aristocrat
lounging on an heirloom couch. Looming things
can kick and scratch. Last night my writing desk—
tucked away on an attic floor—fell through
the wooden slats and landed at my dumb toes.
Thunder blooms like orchids in a black and white
photograph and morphs into the shapes
of fashionable shoes. That last clap
was a lady's laced-up boot, circa 1930.
I want to say *chandelier* just for the muscular
lilt of it, just for the museum rooms
and soap operas of it. Teeth dream their way
through the language they are forced to chew,
but isn't Italian an ensemble of hills
and sautéed truffles? Cymbals
crash all over the cottage roof and dirt flecks
the opaque covers on the soft bed.

NIGHTGOWN

Each night I sleep wrapped in a gown
of crying stars. Whether they cry
to plea or sing is always difficult
and tenuous to decipher. In my gown
of voices, I pitch and roll as if on a ship
at sea. I dream of sisters and brothers;
I dream of stroking my husband's penis,
bright and flushed as an orchid, until
we are interrupted by the blond shores
of windows and the plaintive smell of cut hay,
its disheveled sweetness. The world's a gallery
hung with the obsessive knowledge of light,
light that could be memorizing, as we speak,
one claw foot of the world's daintiest
bathtub. I don't ever want to say *until* again—
it carries too much waiting inside; it is a parade
of soft pelicans procrastinating. In the day,
I pluck music from other poets' poems,
and it falls like tender, snow-covered
fruit into my hands. There is no greater joy.
I want a nightgown woven from the wings
of hummingbirds. Or do I mean from
the birds of humming wings? Or is my nightgown
just a linguistic invention—a cage of syllables
cascading all about me, a rain of *hums*
I wrap around me hungrily?

EXCAVATION

I knew something was horribly wrong
when I awoke, still in my dream, and saw
large, fleshy insects crawling crab-like
on my wall—their bodies a strange,
unaccounted-for blossoming. Then
it turned into a dinner-party,
like in Agatha Christie: the women
in low-backed dresses, as if someone
were slowly pulling a beige window shade
down their backs, the high bird-cage clatter
of their voices.

At this unfolding event,
I'm the host and not yet
properly dressed. Slipping behind
a brocade curtain, I'm putting on my bra
when people begin to trickle
like a silken, sequined liquid
into the room. I'm at a loss
as to what to do, except that I know
there's a man near me I want
to attract. *I wouldn't mind*—I think in my dream—
if he strummed me like a lonely,
Hungarian violin. This is when I place
a black jacket over my shoulders
and begin to greet guests. And this is when,
upstairs in my bedroom,
the insects are multiplying
more fervently than ever.
A Hazmat team has been dispatched
by some unknown, off-scene authority,
and men in white suits sleep in hammocks
strung a few inches above the floor,

which has become viscous with
a bright-green, gelatin substance.
They're waiting it out, waiting to see
what will hatch next: light-infused eggs
or a lapis lazuli sky. Will this dream be an optimist
or a chemist? Events so often elude
our current formulas and speculation.

Downstairs, I'm busy
with small talk: *the fog, your dress,*
that dying wristwatch, and pondering
my appetite for a touch so sensual
it tugs at all corners of all
seven continents of my body, inundates
my skin with a claret of clairvoyant
waters, snaps up my window-blinds
until I'm soaked in Caribbean beaches
of sunlight. But the dream gets
decidedly practical. In the end,
I'm taking leave of my guests
and trying not to fear
the oncoming autumn: its eerie,
rusty eloquence. *It's August,*
I say to myself, almost like a chant,
and as I say it the month buoys up
around me, offering its humid wings,
opening and closing; its panting crickets,
its drifting violins dusty with resin,
and I accept this.

DEAR S—

Saint Sebastian, Saint Theresa, Saint
Africa. A continent is surrounded
by water on most sides. I dine
with forks, spoons and knives
surrounding my dinner plate
at night. It's June and the green
blackens so quickly, the trees like
drugged servants bending their arms
in the evening. How much would you
sacrifice to satisfy an urge? This is the season
of parasols and picnics, strawberries,
sewn up tight as pockets, now softening
their doors open. Each fruit coddles
a secret inside like spies in World War II
movies; something wet and private
that is pried out of them
with sharp, well-photographed
utensils. In second grade, Alexia Larr
wouldn't be my friend
unless I held on my tongue
the peach pit she had slickened
with her saliva. Needless to say,
I still remember the underwater
sliminess of that torture. *Saber* in Spanish
is both *to taste* and *to know*—escargot
scripting its particular knowledge
down your throat. The Mediterranean
Sea is polluted, *sabes tú?* You
have to pick your way through,
so much excrement floating
in that tub-water blue. Despite this,
we found our private cove. The lucid,
wavering windows

the water became—my body slipping
through blue after blue,
shattering the bright panes.

MRS. P. GOES HOUSE-HUNTING

Buzz, buzz, buzz goes the world. We are each in a distortion of our own making. The glass is half whatever, depending on the day you are having—its etches and flaws encompassing the mind's dark hesitations. Mrs. P. went house-hunting. Trees braided in and out of the clouds, pollen fell like ash onto her windshield. At one house, Doreen, the realtor, balanced precariously on a step ladder to see if anyone was home—peering inside: the room loomed like a movie scene after the shooting: stripped walls, carpets curled up like infants, fluorescent lights with cords hanging motionless as the birds and stars in a Miró painting. Bright blue, dimpled tarp half-covered a boat in the backyard. At another home, a blue plastic shark hung near the door— mouth open. An address is something we tattoo quietly onto the self. It whispers its letters and numbers into our breathing until it flies constantly behind us, like the banners planes drag, undulating across the sky. You think a place is home and then it's time to move on. You think you are having a bad day when you begin to envy the bees, spinning around helpless in a puddle on a piece of pavement, the sun dousing them in an early summer glow. You envy the tight little frame that pavement becomes for them. The neat circumference of their pain. Most of the time loss fails to offer the drama required: the elegant heroines smoking cigarettes as their lives dwindle away, the enemy troops marching through the town square. Only Mrs. P. driving from name to name: Cherry Lane, Admiral Street, Possum Hill, and the laundromat a block away.

HEAD COLD

It begins as clouds at the back of the brain—grainy, tenderly bruised
clouds. *I want to be free,* your brain exclaims. *Free from what?* you ask
as you make your way down the corridor: beige light pleading
at the occasional window, blond, shining shapes on the mopped,
smooth floor. But you know what your brain means. You could
duck out now, under the red-embroidered *Exit* sign, take off
for pancakes at noon in a little, off-the-beaten-path café, the bathroom
smelling a little smoky, like a memory you know you have and
have forgotten. The sun notches itself another degree towards
the west. In the Western, it's all railroads and horses, the mountains
like movie-star teeth in all their polished snow. You wish you could
head off this cold like bandits at the mountain pass. It rumbles closer,
velvety and particular, amassing in one corner of your consciousness,
like people outside a theater in the rain—their black umbrellas blooming
all at once. In the end, you give in. The furniture moves a few inches
to the right, the pillow embraces you like a distracted mother. You are
grateful as the silence thickens and grows viscous, pours over you
like a kind syrup. From a certain distance, you can imagine the many
small feet of birds skimming the air above your apartment building.
Or you can imagine your clothes loosening their hold—the sleeves
fluttering more lightly about your wrists, your jeans shuffling like
breezy curtains about your hips. This is not Spain with its olive oil
and tourists. This is not Costa Rica, simmering in its varying shades
of green. This is not even the sandbox you played in as a child—
the damp grains of it sticking to your skin—but it is a place,
and with a nod of your head, your whole body falls in.

NO. 37/NO. 19
(SLATE BLUE AND BROWN ON PLUM)
—Mark Rothko (oil on canvas 1958)

The Blue:

A pensive TV screen at 3AM. A slate blue that hums, fat
thumb-print of mind-dust snowing, floating against
the plum. No fruit here, no tilted vase or precisely
placed mandolin. Just a hat of a color no one
will ever wear, a watchful dusk-eye, frail with constant
looking. A wary flickering. Tin angel pirouetting
and pirouetting; thought-slur slowly subsiding
into its own dim, ashen bracken. Moon-husk,
nightingale blood, Ophelia-moan folded into
this rectangular, opalescent eclipse, this tender theater,
brimmed with a city's after-glow, its neon, back-alley breath.
A masturbation of evenings searching for a home, a sliding
of light on light, of murky slopes, musky and alone.
Lavender-soft sequins of rain. Perfume atomizer
spraying its delicate perspiration: a steel blue hissing;
an indigo tsk-tsking. Molecules astute and aglitter
scatter across this movie-star, world-weary mirror;
this cosmetic nocturne powder—abuzz
with its unsteady gloom, it uneasy, sifting loom.

The Brown:

Snuff box smoldering, a smaller rectangle, a patient
plate the plum bleeds through. Suppressed window.
Still-life halo. A rouge tureen holding cinnamons and
cocoas. Stir and stir what you think your eye sees:
the autumn night grinding its leaves: watch it disintegrate
into a powder that sneezes, a chocolate that breezes.
Lullaby, sleepy decision, sullen gleam; crushed walnut hymn
a child sings to herself, sings and sings. Fat dream-zipper
fastened timidly shut; a fawn-colored forever; a swollen night cup.

LOST EARRING

A poet once told me that he wrote a poem simply
to write a poem—no other premise was required.
I found that freeing. Another poet recently explained
he had decided to study one word for a whole year.
This poet had chosen the word *and.* "How boring,"
I thought, until I paused to assess how much an *and*
can connect: a carrot to a blushing radish; a melodramatic
sadness to a scissor-sharp glee. Even a diamond-studded
bride could be leashed tenuously to a cracked syringe
glittering in a parking lot by applying this one-
syllable conjunction. That's when I realized *and*
was one of the primary colors in the language,
like one of Rothko's blues receding further and further
into his canvas—an unstoppable hallway of blue,
an unraveling cobalt bandage. Each day constructed
from a series of *ands*, a chain-link fence of small mouths
opening: the lost earring shaped like a black tear
my husband gave me, and the wedding I wish
I had attended in northern Spain in my thirties,
with that region's most famous cheese shaped
like a woman's breast, and the trees so dense
they emitted a chartreuse fog in the evenings.

THE SWILL OF SLEEP

"It's sad to fall asleep. It separates people."
—*Jean Seberg, Breathless*

Each body is a bouquet of mishaps
jagged with breath. When we sleep, we tip over
the jar of our dreams and end up
backstroking through the muck of ourselves:
European airports and dark bodies
falling from the sky: the subconscious
an aging perfume giving off its musky odors
and sweating fedoras. Darling, it's sad
to be a soul phyllo-doughed in skin: we breathe
through the apparatus of ourselves
when we wake and when we sleep.
Enmeshed in scars, Aston Martins,
and back lots weedy
with regret, how can we ever
be with anyone
but ourselves? A kiss
is a false conference of voices, a swerve
in the day two faces briefly make;
a shivering bridge
attempting to support
the breath's weight.
Don't get me wrong, I relish
the martini swill of sleep in my mouth:
its smoky lavenders and dusks of daggers,
its sisters and fathers cursing
from behind the brocade curtains.
The mind is always on trial.
Every decision we make a *pas de deux*
we dance alone across a ballroom.
Sleep, darling, is a gash:
a giddy depth we didn't know we had.

DEAR B—

Dear Babushka, dear
ba-ba-ba-boom, dear oh-my-God
don't broil me alive. The world
is a percussive instrument
we strum until we die—*hum, hum*
go the car wheels over the drive;
pluck, pluck the rain sings
for the one-millionth,
bloody time. The feet
earn their calloused soles
and are the saintliest
body part of all—stomp,
stomping along. Dear
Bang on a Can, I like the way
you slap the sunken eye
of the hollow drum. I like your
New York band's underwater,
booming sound. I like the sea's
surface as well—how it's
hard or soft depending
on the distance from which
you choose to approach. Just try
jumping from the Brooklyn Bridge
towards that ruffling,
dark scarf of water
purring beneath. A kiss can be
the softest slap of all, but
I admire the snow, its soft-shoe
shuffle, its Fred-Astaire
panache, as it debonairly dresses
the trees in white, while slickening
the pavement towards
tuxedo black. Blah, blah, blah,

people do go on about whatever
it is they think they know. *Bruno*
was my mother's maiden name—
a brood of Italians from Sicily
settling in a small sea-side,
Rhode Island town,
near the prosperous,
budding, rubber factory.
That factory's been converted
into high-brow, assisted living now—
with pale sconces in the hall
and a recreation
room—a place we almost,
but never did,
send my grandmother to.
Beached-whale, barracuda
sunrise: the world vacillates
between environmental
documentary and James Bond
thriller, but the clouds burst
and explode between genres;
some evenings, splitting the sky
into lavender, melon
and a wintry vanilla.

A SCANDINAVIAN HOTEL
IN COUPLETS

I dreamt I was in a Scandinavian hotel in New York City.
The wallpaper was ruby and gold; the lamplight

gave off a 1930s', Marlene-Dietrich glow. It was evening.
My father was calling for room service. Our family,

all grown up and somehow gathered into this room,
was broke and couldn't afford another night

in this establishment. The bellboy arrived and announced
Scandinavian guests were in the lobby, expecting

to have our room—the one with last resorts dripping
down its gold-embossed walls. How can a dream conjure up

a hotel like that? A hotel honey-glazed with the signatures
of who we are? Our bodies, for instance—how fond

I am of my hands when I think of them. Our family members.
My father willing to sip a cognac until the last moments

before surrender, before he must admit he's outlived
his version of the moving pictures: Orson Welles puffing

on a cigar, pondering his underrated genius.
Or my sister, with her belly-dancer figure

and champagne breasts, jangling her bracelets, her
three-tiered wedding cake of second chances. New York

unfurled its dark flags and incense-filled mirrors
outside our windows, and my brother paced— impatient

with our hesitation in a crisis. But what a voluptuous
panic, what a ripe indecision: me buoyed there, briefly,

with most of my family, as if we were on a cruise liner
of the subconscious—between shores, floating on

just who we were at that moment: our shoes
and haircuts, the damask glow of our skin;

the bellboy having recently left; the phone
dangling in my father's hand.

PINOCCHIO

In the night, I touched my nose and realized it had grown
to twice its length. A transformation had occurred
after I'd put down my novel and switched off
the bed lamp. The novel took place in 1930s' New York
and was all about basement jazz clubs, cigarettes
passed between people like some kind of silkworm currency—
the smoke silvery and soft, dangling lacy tunnels between
their bodies. And then there was the protagonist, with her
clever quips, but I was no protagonist. So why had my nose
nocturnally grown? I discounted cancer since I had always
assumed I would contract a life-threatening disease in a
more supple body part, such as the breasts or colon.
The nose was the china teacup of the body, I thought, *fraught
with delicacy.* Then I counted all the lies I had ever told,
even tiny tremors in truth, such as the belief that I would
never die—each day lived like its own feisty infinity with
expandable walls and translucent leaves, the sky a pair
of silver-blue lungs always breathing in. Come morning,
my nose had returned to its normal length, so I had to wonder
if I transformed every night. What else had I become
between the hours of 1:00 and 3:00 AM? Had I ever been
a giraffe chewing on a star's misshapen light?
Or a scarred victim of an automobile crash
who recovered her *joie de vivre* only after weeks
of gin martinis? Then it dawned on me that I was possibly
a puppet owned by god-knows-who, and life
only breathed through me at sporadic intervals—
in shiny, intermittent, carefully-rationed parcels.

MINIATURE SECRETARY
INCORPORATING A WATCH
—*James Cox (ca. 1766-1772)*

1.

English (but made for the Russian market), this doll-sized desk

sits atop four thumb-sized bulls, who carry it demurely

on their golden backs. Having once been in the collection

of Princess Z. M. Youssoupof in St. Petersburg (1904), it conjures up

the gilt mirrors and hushed corridors of a princess's house, the servants

whispering conspiratorially to themselves. No signs, however, of ever

being held in any kind of hands show on the rosy, marbled agate

of the mini-cabinet doors, on the smoky, sunset hues of the lower,

polished drawers, which will never open as real drawers should. That

time could be so ornately encased (gold frames the sides, swirls across

the blushing facade like a wild, gilded vine); that the clock itself,

the mere size of a half-dollar, could perch, an afterthought, on top

of these delicate upper doors implies a more ebullient view of the hours,

or, at least, a more poetic one in which time is not so much counted

as bedecked with praise like any proper sovereign.

2.

A confectioner's candy, an almost edible delicacy, this object stood

on mantels and night stands, forever ready to offer its exquisite

inventory of details, to feed the voracious eye with filigree

and pasted jewels. Who, in this life, doesn't need a few scattered

pearls, a glistening surface snagging us, at times, to something other

than ourselves? In this case, to something foreign and deliciously

private, something I know I could never fully own except with

the tenuous embrace of my eyes. "Butterflies and flowers that tremble

in the slightest breath of air" parade across the top of "this whimsical

object," which doubles as music box. All Alice-in-Wonderland fanfare

and magician sleights of hand (to wind the clock, a key must be inserted

into a hole hidden beneath a delicate rosette), this secretary accessorizes

time, renders it subordinate by embroidering it with the over-elegance

of a Marie Antoinette dress. Though I'll never know the intimate

facts of the Princess's life—if she loved indifferently or ardently, adored

that clock as much as its maker must have lovingly cupped the pink,

pear-shaped weight in his hands and blown on the intricate, tiny garden of rubies and pearls just to see them respond to his own breath—

it sits now, stilled, in this glass case: an intact, chubby, little history;

a portmanteau, carrying into this century all its requisite mysteries, and,

like so many objects, outliving hardily, and with a certain indifference,

its maker and mistress.

DEAR HOROLOGIST

DEAR HOROLOGIST,

¿Que hora es? I am gardening through time,
the grass turns cold and resistant
at night, the vines frame
phantom windows, reflecting
the mind's chemical-soaked
images: an old classroom lined
with cabinets rusting at the hinges. A wine,
distilled from resin, drunk in Naples (that city
choked with crumbling windowsills),
which a friend offers to us
on his verandah. Cities come
and go like flashbacks
in the movies—Big Ben's
intricate moon-eye peering out
over sooty traffic. Passport photo-
booths puffing with the camera's
darling magic. Joseph Cornell
pieced together his Europe
by running fingers through
Manhattan's secondhand
bookstores. Ballerinas
cramped like crushed foil
in his star-stuttered boxes. Dalí
allowed his clocks to drip like
milk on an infant's lip. Dear me,
how the mind slips. They say
we are in for some serious
hurricanes. Tape the windows
against the future. In 1938, people
sat on their verandahs
as the waves darkened
and crescendoed like grand pianos.

UPON RETURNING FROM OUR TENTH WEDDING ANNIVERSARY VACATION

There's a bat in the sink—
a three-inch black umbrella
filling then unfilling with breath,
an accordion unaccordioning
itself. When my husband pokes
with the chimney stick,
it squeaks, helpless as a rubber toy
stepped on in the bath. Through the trees,
the train moans on the tracks,
swallowing the slow, dark gravel
of evening. The windows seem chilly,
the bed sheets damp. No more honeysuckle
draping its tendrils over the wild green brush,
no more dunes and their slender paths—
the sand a soft, slipping floor your body
could lounge along and trust. In this life,
small cruelties pile up. The cruelty of leaving
the flue open, so the tender-bodied (yet toothed)
bat could slip down that dark expanse. The cruelty
of not knowing how to handle a half-dead
bat, hunkered down in the drain. So with
the chimney utensils, my husband has no choice
but to bash him on the head, to make him
that much more dead. This is not the way
we wanted to come home, driving away
from the pier, the sunset like watermelon running
its pale juice down the sky, the clouds like hammocks,
swinging long and slow, catching the pinks
and yellows in the stretched braids of their gentle
ropes. Harmony seems a collision of luck

and choice. At least I chose you—
the only man I could watch kill a helpless,
forlorn bat and then welcome,
without a doubt, back into my bed.

THE ELECTRICIAN

I'm cousin to the sun, a hired
cure for darkness. My fingers
busy as rain. In my palms I hold
an invisible, melancholy silence,
a violin with no strings. I stretch
and preen in the shadows,
a pensive, swivel-hipped owl.
I've crawled
into crawl spaces thinner
than a thimble. I finger
the wormy wires, un-cup
the fixtures and peer
at their sex. I know what grows,
furtive as thought, in the porous
walls of houses. I step lightly
through the coffin
cough of attics and closets, among
the boxes, water-stained
and slumped in garages. I coax light
back into rooms, using screw drivers,
flashlights and sleight-of-hand—a stooped,
everyman's magician. On certain
oblique afternoons, I've mirrored
your neglected interiors back at you.

A HISTORY OF APPLES

The lisp of lapels, Mary Astor smoothing down her lover's

ruffled expectations; the ship listing leeward in the lavender bottle

in the bath—you flicking your index finger against the glass

to keep your childhood from heeling too much

to one side. *Correction*: There was no bottle; there were,

however, a few tipsy hopes and you in a skiff,

with a breeze that muttered in Latin, and one warbler

that alighted on your shoulder, tired from flying

over the sea. Was the warbler tired? Or your shoulder?

This is not a novel, but it is the beginning of a history,

a groggy personal tract. Will I die without ever remembering

the exact first apple I placed in my mouth—was it red (I wrote *read*)

or as bright as a green grape? How old was I

and in what state? See how easily geographies and facts drop away,

like the exact color of my mother's house, being repainted as I speak.

We argue over whether to call it *buff* or *shell*, as if the name will change

the color, while on Fifth Avenue a basilica struts through the air, unrepentant as black tobacco. The breathing in of a city. At 20, Paris

perplexed me: that indifferent snowy gray falling in the buildings' stone,

that perpetual mute storm. Out of what quarries did the French dig

such stubborn clouds, out of what sanctimonious declivities? Each

metropolis is built on coincidence, on invisible, succulent slippages;

each life a seam in a silk stocking snagging unexpectedly. Summer

now exhibits its casual calculus; a humid lesson in diminishing returns.

Slice and slice away at its plump shape—the trees coughing up mist,

the sun, a swollen lozenge, dissolving on your tongue—and witness

how a season gives up its travel itineraries as easily as Havana hiccups

cigars. *Bon voyage!* Let's clink to that, to the arrival of the next moment,

whether we want it or not; to the mauve ice in our vodka tonics;

and to the limes: inquisitive, unblinking, ready for anything.

A CARIBBEAN CALENDAR

The body is a podium the weather
steps up to. There, the blue-haired rain
swung its hips across the verandah one afternoon, but mostly
it was sun as hot as a cigarette—a vague smokiness
we got used to, a steam-room strut the sun did
from morning to dusk. Occasionally, there were whiffs
of gasoline, electricity blackouts—our living room
blind as ink. The sea was its own machine: a silky
engine-purr of blues and greens, an automatic sheen
to the well-paced waves batting their Egyptian eyelids.
A green respiration flowered deep in the water
whenever I looked down at my feet—pale and backlit
against the blond sand, the undulating floor. Things uttered
to themselves: the birds; the palm trees with their moppy,
dry tops—the fronds slapping heavily against each other
in the husky, off-season wind.

A novice at such hothouse geographies, I never
had my snorkeling gear on hand, so the sea remained
a sketchy blur mumbling around my ears, a rippling
encyclopedia offering its bright shapes and colors
at a lonely distance. I only knew the name for one flower:
the *bougainvillea*, whose pinwheels easily waterfalled
about me: indigo, magenta, blue and blood-orange stars
pouring delicately from bushes and trees, as if blooms
were cocktails to be sipped matter-of-factly. For a time,
I was licked clean. The sun scoured my skin, the rum awoke
in my blood and sashayed and strummed. Our last night,
just like a child, I said bye to the moon, to its sad,
wide stupor, its swollen glow:
our one Caribbean week was over.

DEAR V—

Dear vellum, dear viceroy,
dear Vermeer and the eerie light
that can be found edging
around our lives. The missing persons
spilling out of our mail each night.
The broken neon glow
of a highway I once drove
on my way to a twelve-egg omelet
folded into a neat blanket
perched softly on my plate. Landscapes
pile up in a life—not India, not Africa,
but Venice, its ankle-deep waters
I splashed through after a storm,
or The Cloisters in upper Manhattan,
all medieval France and Spain
tucked inside a verdant estate, not far off
the squeaking brakes of the MTA. Dear
Venezuela, dear *will I ever get out of here?*,
a cage is a place our lungs
breathe out of, each breath a missive
to the sky above. I prayed hard
when I was ten years old, but the evenings blurred
just the same into a postcard Dutch landscape
of purple and gray. Faith is known
for its cornucopia of forms: an image
of the Virgin burned into a peasant's shirt,
Jesus' watery profile stamped onto a spoon,
and Santa Teresa's finger
saved in a glass case—the mossy softness
of the bone, the ring glittering
at its base. In my mother's book on world art,
Botticelli's Venus rose from the waters
on her pearly shell—her skin serene

as an unmade bed, her vagina covered
by her tresses of drifting red hair. I scratched and scratched
in my diaries as a child—cream-colored pages
stuffed beneath my bed each night, but if you asked,
I would say film directors have it made.
They place a filter over the lens and *Voila!!*
their world is transformed into a coppery,
late-October glow. I've often wished
I could do that in a poem, watch
the stain of my intent
seep into the window frames,
the protagonist's arms, the hotel room's
purring vents.

POIROT

Could a mustache really be an ink spill
fastidiously pruned on a man's face? Who
knew Belgium could produce a parcel
of gray-paisley ties, spats and patent leather
shoes shining so sprightly a cabaret girl
could coif her hair in their twin
black mirrors? His chest a Cornell box
of silk vests, bow ties and turn-
of-the-century buttons—a dandy's scarf
winking from a jacket's pocket. If murder knew
its adversary would be a perennial bachelor
with OCD, would it ever relax its jagged
tools and relentless blood, now pooling
like a rose-colored dahlia across a woman's
breast? How matter-of-factly he now stands,
poised over the beauty who drank the wrong gin.

COMPARISONS

Hibiscus loafers brushed as soft
as a baby's tongue

versus flesh-toned $99 sandals—
gold-buckled. The gray

pitch-perfect words
buried in a gray-bird's

sloping breast
versus the unspoken syllable

that weighs, a whole afternoon
of unfallen rain,

in my May mouth.
I hold up one blue

against another: each blue
is selfish, sips its fluorescent

cocktail, and shuns
comparisons: Persian blue

does not exist for periwinkle; an iris
will not bed down happily

with an azure. I only know today
from yesterday. I only know those roses

are clocks sagging dark faces
into bright grass.

Does the memory
of a cup of coffee—

its absolute authority
on my tongue—

bear any resemblance to the drop
of red cardinal now bobbing on the tree's

pert branch? Does nostalgia equal
blue stucco houses in a Moroccan village

I will never visit? All equations
are false, or at least prone

to slipperiness. Each minute grows
stranger and more fragrant—

white-breasted squirrels drop,
as if on cue, from bitter-green

bickering trees, the neighborhood smells
of lavender wisteria and printer ink,

and fishermen along the inlet
can't catch the fish that swim

like pale, separate hands
in the dark waters

three feet beneath them.

TODAY, I AM NOT

a 23-year-old woman
holding a lime-colored,

perspiring cocktail
in a nightclub with black

octagonal mirrors. I'm not
the word asleep in my husband's

mouth as a dark bird lifts
packages of bright

wind on its somber,
steadfast back. I'm not

myself at 20—a tilted,
unblinking match

flaring down the black
of a British night,

confident I will spot
the hostel up ahead.

I am not a shoe, a *shush*
or a *shut-up*. Meanwhile, the rose

pirouettes and scuttles
on its stem—a pink crab with soft,

flirting claws and vivacious
thoughts. Today, edges scold

and blur, so I lean
into charcoal algorithms

and bleeding
clouds. I'm not decisive,

not a precise record-keeper
of animal or plant life. Saxophones

hum and sweat
among the clairvoyant

petunias and lavender
phlox. I am not

a fox—all sleek, nocturnal
journal-keeping and inky

footprints in the purple
grass. What a gas it is

to be an extra in a film—to populate
rainy cities and street corners

with your pale arms and
blurry sins! I am not

my whims, my short-winded
whistle, my steamer trunk

of sequined fears. I am not
an aptly peeled pear.

TULIPS ARE FOUND TO BE ONE OF THE MOST DELICIOUS FOODS IN THE ANIMAL WORLD

The dark pink windowpanes of the tulips
shattered and splayed on the April grass,
as if a nocturnal crime had occurred, a small crime, a crime
with parentheses around it. My husband set out
like an underpaid sleuth to figure it out. He read
on the internet about tulips and the appetites
of animals. He called his mother, an experienced
Texas farmer. Had it been a deer who ate those gelatos
of cinnamon and rose that had dripped their *Italy* and *Rome*
down the air in front of our rented cottage? A pale cottage
thrown carelessly against the side of a hill, like a discarded shell
given up by the nearby harbor (the rooms long and introverted;
the kitchen painted the shallow green of a swimming pool).
But during the night (a warmish one with stars full of relief
and regret in equal degree), we hadn't heard any clopping
of hooves up our yard's uneven stone stairs, assuming
deer's hooves *clop*. The other options: a squirrel or rabbit.
For some reason, we couldn't imagine either jumping that high—
the tulips had been rather tall—and adeptly devouring
each furled house of color, each ragged fist of coral and peach,
each tipsy convent of kept light tottering
on top of the stem. Some blooms had disappeared altogether—
the green stalks truncated, as if having undergone a sixteenth-
century beheading. Or had it been a slow
undressing? The flowers unzipped by the larger night,
a knowledge they hadn't bargained for come for them—
their dresses in tattered folds on the chilled morning ground.

In the end, we gave in and let the headless stalks persist. There was a shut
sadness to their blind vigil, an ascetic's pride. They lingered,
as certain losses can, enduring longer than their original beauty,
and held their scarred peace with the spring.

HISTORY LESSON

Sluggish oceans lick away at my heart, its watery, weighted bells,
but the wind is beginning to kick up.

It's the season of bees. Swaddled in heat, they're little
scribes of daylight; their bodies
buoy on the breeze as they sniff and sniff
but never sneeze.

A season is like a classroom with sealed windows, the sun
shifting its cinnamon brocade arms across the grass.
You're inside, unable to guess the exact time
dusk will arrive.

Bees categorize the air, but into what categories, into what
shivering columns of insight?

Can I have a sip of espresso, please? But, waiter, it must
be from a café in Milan in 1985—the January rain
pooling in my shoes, the beige sleep from a cheap
hotel folded into the cup like a wasp's wing.

Arguments slough off reason like a dancing girl erupting
out of a birthday cake—clumps of bright frosting
collapsing onto the floor.

And birthdays accrue—an abacus slung onto our backs
like a bow and arrow, a constant weaponry we lug around.
Where's the hero to rescue us from
such diligent record keeping?

I don't care what anyone says: Turkish coffee
is like Brooklyn in mid-August, the pavement softened
into black tar, time no longer on your side.

At 45, what stream am I rowing down? What coordinates
do I possess? Maps suggest you can crisscross
from one continent to the next, with no cost to yourself.

But on a map, a mountain is a blur of green seagulls;
the Alps are slender Audrey Hepburns smoking cigarettes
and never contracting lung cancer, are silver-winged
butterflies pinned to white construction paper.

Every distance I've meandered
resides in me, wringing its stubborn hands
so when I bleed, I bleed away where I have been: salty
stairways in Lisbon, revolving doors
in a modern museum, French fountains
drunk on themselves.

What is confidence but a bunch of honeyed
slippery bricks—bees wax melting into my hands
when, *tsk, tsk,* the day didn't go as I planned,
when the north wind gossiped
hard against my skin.

HOW TO SURVIVE YOURSELF: NINE STEPS

(for Claudia Emerson)

1. When you start taking yourself too seriously, think of whales—
   the dark secrets of water they swim through, the envelopes
   of ocean they open with their toothless, bristled mouths.

2. Read a poem in which you learn baleen whales were hunted once
   for those bristled mouths—the coarse hairs used for corsets,
   umbrellas, brushes, brooms. The hardware of a whale's mouth
   lived among men and women whenever it rained, whenever
   a woman brushed her hair or breathed out.

3. Think of your own hair. How, when you moved from your last
   apartment, you had to sweep the corners and floors and were
   amazed at its persistence: dusty strands and *S*'s curling around
   chair legs, wild grasses swaying beneath beds; skies of it clouding
   over doors and portholes, shy locks clinging to the edges of
   night-tables and beds.

4. If that doesn't work, say *corset* five thousand times until it morphs
   into *core, ore, galore*—an ocean of sound much larger than
   you could ever worry about.

5. Try not to panic if the evening turns a bitter abrupt green, if the
   clouds are bruised apples tumbling towards you, and you fear
   you won't be able to catch a world wider than you.

6. Be grateful for small survivals: the dimple of blue the bluebird
   flies through—that slit in the day, that vial of violet. Don't worry
   if your words sound over-poetic or sing too trillingly. What is
   a *trill*, anyway? A thrilled sound? A leaky lullaby stuck inside
   a bird's mouth?

7. Invite a friend over for a drink and toast to husbands and violins, to the novels you'll never read: their restless heroines, their badly-lit stairwells and awkward conversations, the names of their meandering, snow-encrusted fields.

8. And, if certain words you once loved elude you, adopt new ones like siblings you never had, like a troupe of performers encircling you, building their archipelago of patient sound: *ochre, aver, circumvolution.*

9. Finally, if all else fails, sidle up alongside the stars in someone else's poem, stars guiding them on a night drive to Texas. Learn from those stars, from their sleepy-eyed tolerance, from their sluggish whale-like swim through the dark.

MY LIFE AS A DESSERT

At ten, it was the meringue
your mother carefully prepared—a puffy,
delicately-crusted concoction,
a hill your spoon chipped away at
like an excavation, only to find
sugar and air inside. Who could stomach
such a mountain of frivolous delight?
You could, until you were fifteen.
Then the sugar stung
your teeth and gums,
and you knew that time in your life,
the meringue period, was done.
Now (you assert) you are more
than the sum of your desserts: the brownies
and homemade chocolate chip cookies—
the uncooked dough stuffed into a glass,
saved in the fridge for when your brother
got home from soccer practice, a family ritual
no one questioned. The sweet tooth
syrupy and smooth as any trait
in the gene pool. You are even more
(you claim) than the apple strudel
once offered to you
by a kindly German couple
on a train ride through the Alps
(the mountains outside
whispery and patient as a
flour-dusted brioche); more than
the rugelach you purchased
one evening in New York—
their dark chocolate a slick path
your tongue searched along,
a trip to a foreign country
you never bothered to name.

Now, outside the commuter train
the night stirs around you. Orange street lights
swerve in and out of sight. Long Island
seems a festooned *magdalena*,
as the Spanish would say: a slender,
finger-shaped pastry,
a geography your mind
slowly eats through. You have never
trusted a film in which
the heroine neither eats nor drinks.
Panic and crisis, even despair
need caffeine, need a little sugar
spooned into the scene. Childhood
was an extravaganza, food-dyed
and mossy-green. Could any chef
build with custards and tarts
those brackish muddy brooks,
the warm, fertile smell of dusk
and summer asphalt? You are
(you concede) the sum of your desserts,
only if by desserts one means a trembling
catalogue of hopes and concerns
or the occasional, indelible memory:
the velvety flan, for instance,
that waited for you
one afternoon in a café in Madrid—
like it knew you would arrive
just at that particular place and time:
a milky sun ready to die
slowly on your tongue.

I'VE DECIDED TO WRITE THE GREATEST POEM IN THE WORLD

It will encompass the mother-of-pearl glow of the Caribbean
and the best latté I ever sipped, which was in a café
bordering a sloping plaza in Siena, Italy. There will be
tendrils in this poem, green shoots growing out of
its spine, and an occasional rose so soft and brimming
anyone would swear it was a champagne glass
they could sip demurely from, and with each taste,
pain would evaporate, such as a six-year-old getting shot
outside the local library and breast cancer feasting on
the 21st century, female body. I don't think I will insert
scoliosis into this poem. My mother might make a brief
appearance: her right pinky finger bent since birth,
so that her hand always seems to be holding a teacup
when it isn't—that hand half-curled around a shapely
emptiness. I will lay, side-by side, like knives in a velvet
drawer, the nights my husband and I made love with the
nights we didn't. Myrna Loy will make a cameo appearance—
martini shaker in her evening hands. There will be a gaggle
of detectives, and someone will finally be proven innocent.
The trees won't succumb and the houses won't give, no matter
the speed and mood of the green wind, and the tea I pick up
in my hands will smell of vanilla extract and a ten-year-old
about to blow softly into his piccolo.